Look - Book 2
VI

By Viola & Zaida Stefano

The rights of Viola & Zaida Stefano to be identified as the authors of this work have been asserted by them in accordance with the **Copyright Amendment (Moral Rights) Act 2000.**

All rights reserved. Apart from any use as permitted by the authors & under the **Copyright Act 1968**, no part may be reproduced, copied, scanned, stored in a retrieval system, recorded, or shared, by any means or in any form, without prior written permission from the publisher.

A catalogue record of this book is available from the **National Library of Australia.**

ISBN: 978-0-6458056-9-7

Authors: Viola Stefano & Zaida Stefano
Illustrations, cover & internal designs: Zaida Stefano

Illustrations copyright © Zaida Stefano 2023
Design copyright © Zaida Stefano 2023

Disclaimer: The content presented in this book is meant for educational purposes only. The authors & publisher claim no accountability to any entity or person for any liability, damage, or loss caused or assumed to be caused directly or indirectly as a consequence of the application, use, or interpretation of the material in this book.

VeeZee Publications

Copyright © VeeZee Publications Pty Ltd 2023
First published in Australia in 2023
by VeeZee Publications Pty Ltd
veezeepublications.com

Learning made easy with

VeeZee!

- Focus Core words in 'Look - Book 2' and the 'Look' series (yellow)
- Secondary Core words in 'Look - Book 2' and the 'Look' series (blue)
- Other secondary Core words in the 'Look' series but **NOT** in 'Look - Book 2' (green)

Core Vocabulary used throughout **VeeZee Publications**				
I	want	can	stop	look
like	more	he	go	see
here	what	do	the	and
out	where	we	it	up
not	they	when	that	down
she	now	them	is	put
help	off	you	yes	on
turn	who	this	no	why
done	make	a	to	under
come	in	some	which	there
open	get	good	same	home

Supporting students with low vision (vision impairment - VI)

Our VI range has been especially developed to give children with low vision the very best opportunity to learn. The illustrations in the VI version of the readers, replicate key elements of the photographs included in the other version of the readers. We have done this so that all students engage with the same content. Yellow framing is used around each illustration to support children with low vision to focus on the illustrations more readily. Each book is carefully designed with deliberate and strategic use of colour, background and contrast for typescript and for illustrations. Placing these colours onto a black background supports children with low vision to see the illustrations more successfully because of the contrast provided. Teachers should provide guidance to their students by talking about the colours, lines and themes of each illustration. Ask questions using Core words; who, what, where, when and why, to reinforce their associations with surrounding words. The illustrations with their vibrant colours included in our VI range have been created to promote student interest, engagement and learning. Please ensure that classroom lighting provides optimal conditions for students to engage with the VI readers. We advise that students without a vision impairment also explore the readers designed for students with low vision. This will support interaction and discussion amongst the students. It is our hope that this will ultimately promote acceptance, understanding, compassion and teamwork, thus cultivating true inclusion.

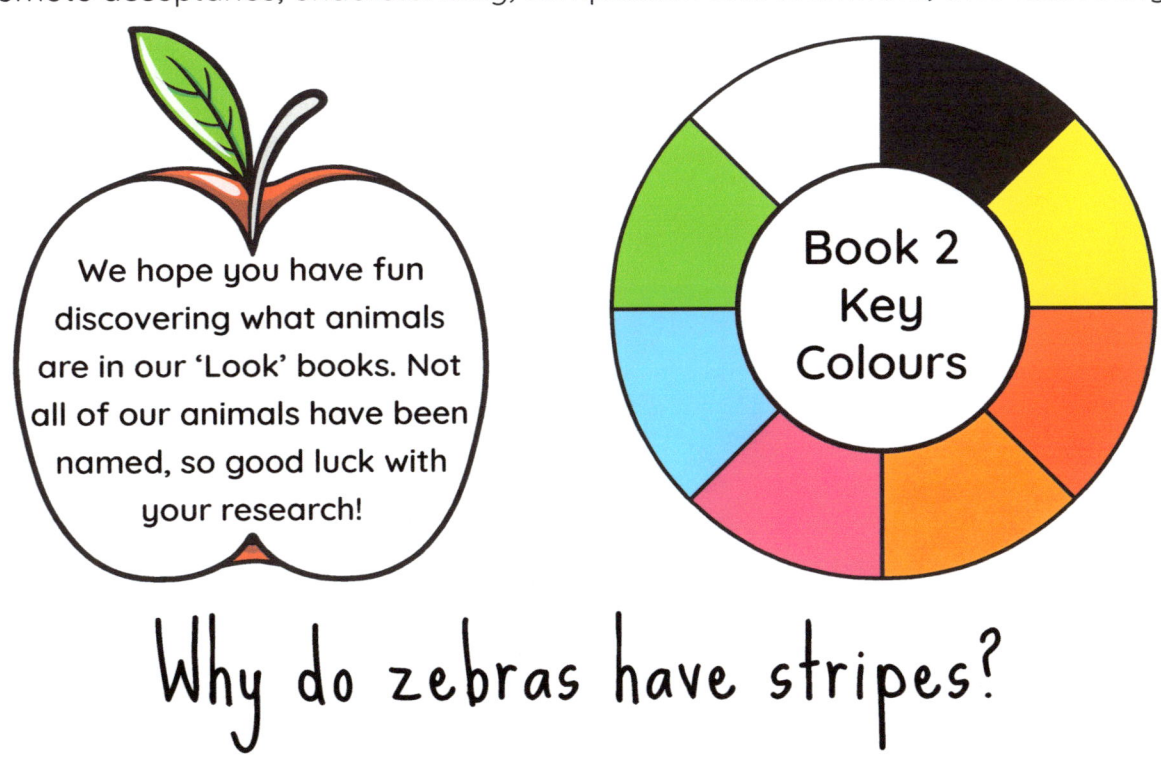

We hope you have fun discovering what animals are in our 'Look' books. Not all of our animals have been named, so good luck with your research!

Book 2 Key Colours

Why do zebras have stripes?

Look.

Look here and look there.

Come look here.

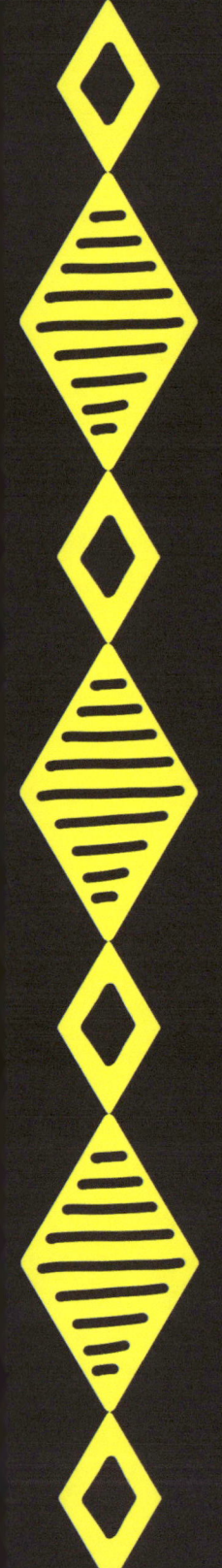

Look. Come look here mum and dad.

Turn left and look here.

Turn right and look there.

Turn left and look here now.

Turn right and look there now.

Look. I can see it.

Look at it.

Look. Can you see it?

Look. I can see them.

Look. Can you see them?

Look. I can see it here.

Look. I can see them there.

30

Look mum and dad. We can see them.

Words in this book

look	I	can
here	there	turn
come	now	them
	it	

Words in this book

and	at	left
right	mum	dad
see	we	you

Do you know the focus and secondary Core words: 'look', 'here' and 'I'? Read the words along each line.

look	here	look	look	I	look	here
I	look	here	look	here	I	look
look	I	look	here	look	I	look
here	look	I	look	here	look	here
look	here	look	look	here	I	look
look	here	I	look	I	look	here
here	I	here	I	look	here	look

Do you know the focus and secondary Core words in this book (refer to Core word table)? Find them along each line, point to them and say them. Read the other words too once you have pointed to the Core words.

I	there	look	at	dad	them	mum
here	look	turn	come	now	look	you
it	you	we	look	can	and	see
right	look	there	can	look	them	look
left	I	look	here	and	see	right
look	turn	we	now	look	them	mum
you	look	look	come	we	look	at

How many times did you read the word 'look'?

Make new words with '__ight', e.g., 'light'. Write sentences using these words.

We hope you had fun reading!

VeeZee Publications

Wait, there's more!

Visit our website for information about our range of readers & supporting products.

veezeepublications.com

www.ingramcontent.com/pod-product-compliance
Lightning Source LLC
Chambersburg PA
CBHW050853010526
44107CB00047BA/1593